T5-BYT-555

Gatherings
Small Group Ministry for Men

Tony Bushman and Bill Hamilton-Holway

Skinner House Books
Boston

Copyright © 2006 by F. Anthony Bushman and William P. Hamilton-Holway. All rights reserved.
Published by Skinner House Books, an imprint of the Unitarian Universalist Association of
Congregations, a liberal religious organization with more than 1,000 congregations in the U. S. and
Canada. 25 Beacon Street, Boston, MA 02108-2800.

Printed in the United States.

ISBN 1-55896-514-9
978-1-55896-514-0

10 9 8 7 6 5 4 3 2 1
09 08 07 06

Library of Congress Cataloging-in-Publication Data

Bushman, Tony.
  Gatherings : small group ministry for men / by Tony Bushman and Bill
Hamilton-Holway.
      p. cm.
   ISBN-13: 978-1-55896-514-0 (pbk. : alk. paper)
   ISBN-10: 1-55896-514-9 (pbk. : alk. paper) 1. Worship programs. 2.
Church group work with men. I. Hamilton-Holway, Bill. II. Title.

BV199.M43B87 2006
259.081—dc22

2006016534

We gratefully acknowledge permission to reprint the following materials:
"This Day Is Mine" by Raymond J. Baughan, used by permission of William F. Baughan.
"Anxiety" and "Each of Us Is an Artist" by Arthur Graham, used by permission of Betty Graham.
Excerpt from *Seasons of the Soul* by Robert T. Weston, used by permission of Dick Weston.

Contents

Introduction

Gatherings is a ritualized series of eight small-group worship services offering men an opportunity to grow spiritually and personally by meeting in an atmosphere of appreciation, attentive listening, and self-discovery. Through shared leadership and participation, Gatherings nurtures a culture of trust and support.

Over the many years that we have been doing pastoral work, both with individuals and in support groups, we have found that certain issues continually arise among men. We have also found that men often feel most secure talking about these issues when they are sharing them with other men because there is a feeling of common experience and understanding. This program is designed to provide an outlet for men to explore together what it means to be men and to give and receive support. Respect, safety, and mutual regard grow as men share their experiences, feelings, doubts, and hopes.

Although an individual may lead a Gatherings program, we recommend co-leaders. Sharing this role models mutuality and enables each leader, at times, to step back and observe the group dynamics. Sharing leadership is easier, less risky, more flexible, and more fun than working alone. While choosing leaders with experience in group facilitation is recommended, inexperienced leaders can be successful simply by following the orders of service and reading the suggestions for leaders at the end of this book. Participants may wish to continue meeting beyond the eight gatherings, with a new team assuming responsibility for leadership.

Some participants may have babysitters at home or early morning commitments. It is important to honor the two-hour schedule for the gathering, beginning and ending on time. If time is running out in any gathering, the group may decide to go beyond the closing time, but only if all participants agree. Regular attendance makes for a strong group. If you know you will miss a meeting, let the leader or another member of the group know in advance.

At the end of this book, you will find exercises that form the basis for Communing at each gathering. The preparation time is usually about twenty minutes. Preparing in advance by writing or drawing your responses to the questions eliminates the need to do the preparatory exercises during the meeting and maximizes the time available for sharing. Your group may use a buddy system to encourage completion of exercises and nurture the development of relationships among participants. Your group may begin each gathering by talking through the Order of Service. Some of you may volunteer to lead different parts as you move through the services. Each Order of Service contains the following elements: a Chalice Lighting, Opening Words, two songs, Sharing Joys and Sorrows, readings, a period of silence, Communing, sharing feelings or appreciations, and Closing Words.

Chalice Lighting and Opening Words

Words for lighting the chalice and Opening Words are provided in each order of service, but your group may choose to use a favorite Chalice Lighting ritual from your congregation instead. The Chalice Lighting and Opening Words can be spoken by one person or in unison.

Songs

Each Order of Service includes a song after the Opening Words and a song near the end of the service. Most of the songs have been chosen from *Singing the Living Tradition*, the hymnal of the Unitarian Universalist Association.

Sharing Joys and Sorrows

Each Order of Service includes a time for sharing joys and sorrows with silent support. While this element is important for each man to be able to let go of the concerns of the day in order to be fully present with the group, it should be brief so that it does not exhaust the available time. Not everyone needs to speak, though at the first gathering every man should at least introduce himself.

Readings

Each gathering includes two kinds of readings. The first kind of reading occurs right after Sharing Joys and Sorrows. The words are either provided in the Order of Service or can be found in *Singing the Living Tradition*. Your group may divide into two parts for this reading.

The second type of reading is called Readings from the Common Bowl. After each Order of Service, you will find a collection of quotations on the theme of the Gathering. Before the Gathering, photocopy these quotations, cut them up into individual slips of paper, and place them in a bowl. Participants will each select quotations at the Gathering until none is left. Each person will read his quotation(s) while everyone listens. The quotations have been selected to represent a diversity of views, so that each person's truth may be represented. If there are more quotations than men in the group, participants can be invited to select the quotation that speaks most profoundly to them.

Sitting in Silence

Everyone is invited to remain quiet for two minutes, preparing to listen to one another. A volunteer can offer some words like, "Our attentive listening to one another is a way to show love and create the Beloved Community," or "Let us begin our sharing, showing our care for one another through our attentive listening." One of you may want to ring a bell at the end of two minutes as a way of drawing people back to the group.

Communing

People's life stories and feelings are personal and sacred, containing deep material worthy of the group's regard, full respect, and gratitude. Communing, the major event of each gathering, offers an opportunity for each person to speak without interruption while others listen attentively. It is not a time for questions or comments. If someone does comment, you may choose to let the silence of the group reestablish the norm of quiet listening. If conversation begins, remind yourselves that this is a time of quietly taking in what each speaker has to offer.

The person speaking will often discover himself going deeper than he imagined, discovering new truths within himself. If he seems troubled or sheds tears, do not rush in to say anything; what he is experiencing may be beneficial for him. If you sense that support is appropriate, you might offer gentle, comforting words such as, "Take your time. We're here to listen." Sometimes just a simple "thank you" will suffice.

Rather than proceeding around the circle, people should be invited to speak when they feel moved to do so. There may be an awkward silence before anyone speaks or between speakers, but these quiet times don't always have to be filled. Sometimes "silence is golden," and necessary to digest what is happening as the group learns to be together in a new and deep way.

The number of men in the group and the time remaining in the gathering will determine how much time each man has to share. While each may have more to share than time allows, keep in mind that we give each other a gift when we speak succinctly. Depending upon how long people speak, there may be a second opportunity for people to add anything that was forgotten or something that was stirred by others' sharing, but this is still not a time for discussion, feedback, or debate.

Appreciations

As the gathering draws to a close, each person will have the chance to briefly name any feelings or express appreciation for what he just experienced.

Following the gathering, some people may linger to speak informally and directly with each other or with the leader. While this time is not part of the two-hour gathering, it can be an important opportunity to deepen relationships.

We hope that you enjoy Gatherings. We have done our best to present a program that has integrity and meaning, but the idea behind it is to encourage participants to really listen to and be present with each other and with themselves. With this guiding principle in mind, we encourage you to adapt the elements of this program to your group's particular needs and desires. May your time together enrich your understanding and be a blessing to you.

Getting to Know One Another

Chalice Lighting

At times our own light goes out and is rekindled by a spark from another person. Each of us has cause to think with deep gratitude of those who have lighted the flame within us.
—*Albert Schweitzer*

Opening Words

We gather together to share our lives,
 to be together as men seeking to live more fully.
We gather together to meet one another
 to grow and show our respect.
Here let us make room for ourselves and one another
 by listening with appreciation
 and speaking directly.
Come, let us worship.

Song

Grace guide us now as we begin,
Make manifold the love within,
Speak through our lips, hear through our ears,
Touch all our longing, calm our fears.

(to the tune of "Old Hundredth," Hymn 371 in *Singing the Living Tradition*)

Sharing Joys and Sorrows

Please speak as you feel moved.

Reading

What exactly do men seek today?
 We want healthier ways of relating to women, other men, and the children in our lives.

We want work large enough to stretch our minds and touch our hearts.

> We want male support so that we can exchange delights, wounds, impasses, and longings in a safe, caring atmosphere.

For what do men yearn today?

> We want to quit having to prove ourselves at the office, in bed, and on the playing field so that we can begin to let go, relax, and reveal our true selves.

We want to be strong but not macho, gentle without being wimpish, vulnerable without falling prey to self-pity, both needy and self-reliant, expressive rather than emotionally constricted, more spiritually awake.

> We want to be mature enough that we don't always have to seem mature.

What do we want for ourselves and for other men?

> We want to grow bolder as we age: shedding habits, taking risks, claiming our rights.

—Tom Owen-Towle

Readings from the Common Bowl   *Take turns reading aloud.*

Sitting in Silence   In the quiet, may we be in touch with what we want to say to these people on this day.

Communing   *This is the heart of our service. Take turns sharing an exciting, interesting, or meaningful time of your life.*

Song   "From You I Receive," Hymn 402 in *Singing the Living Tradition*

Giving Thanks   We give thanks for the gifts of each other's sharing.
We say, "Thank you for risking your story.
Thank you for creating a place of safety.
Thank you for listening with appreciation."
As we deepen our knowing of one another through the weeks
to come,

May we claim the male nature within us.
May we find strength and gentleness,
Companionship, and hope for the future.

Closing Words

As it was tonight, sharing our lives, showing our respect, may it be so in all the weeks to come.

Readings from the Common Bowl

If it is language that makes us human, one half of language is to listen. Silence can exist without speech, but speech cannot live without silence. Listen to the speech of others. Listen even more to their silence.

—Jacob Trapp

You can't eat for eight hours a day nor drink for eight hours a day nor make love for eight hours a day—all you can do for eight hours is work. Which is probably the reason why we make ourselves and everybody else so miserable and unhappy.

—attributed to William Faulkner

All life is an experiment. The more experiments you make the better. What if you are a little course, and you may get your coat soiled or torn. What if you do fail and get fairly rolled in the dirt once or twice? Up again, you shall never be so afraid of a tumble.

—Ralph Waldo Emerson

At some moment I did answer *Yes* to Someone—or Something—and from that hour I was certain that existence is meaningful and that, therefore, my life, in self-surrender, had a goal.

—Dag Hammarskjold

I wish to learn what life has to teach, and not, when I come to die, discover that I have not lived.

—Henry David Thoreau

We enter the territory of the heart by going into our wounds and reliving them. By "wounds" I mean those blows from life that stun and injure one's spirit or lacerate and mark the tissues of the soul. There are three major sources of wounds for men: the hurts suffered in childhood, the blows received in initiatory circumstances, and the losses in life that become the cloth of the cloaks of the elders. The eye of initiation sees darkly and sees in the darkness of suffering the glint of survival and the glimmer of emerging wisdom.

—Michael Meade

Life is like an onion: you peel one layer at a time, and sometimes you weep.

—Anonymous

Male identity is very strongly linked to personal actions, decisions, ideas, and facts.

—Cris Evatt

Why do you like a sunset? Why do you like to make money? What is money for? What was the last book you read? Do you have any friends? What is a friend anyway? Do you like your children? Do you sometimes smile or laugh in public at your shortcomings? Do you have any shortcomings? Has making love ever been a religious experience for you? If not, what went wrong? When you wake up in the morning, are you eager and pleased to begin another new day? If not, what's wrong? What do you long for above all else? What do you want?

—James Curtis

It isn't what you have, but what you are, that makes life worthwhile.

—Anonymous

The pillars of male identity are warfare, work and sex.

—*Sam Keen*

Feminist women have been actively searching out the relationships between their sexualities and their spiritualities. Their discoveries have been illuminating—indeed exciting. They have found that what they have experienced as women and as females is of enormous significance in understanding their relationships to God, the world, others, and themselves. We who are men are starting to realize that the same is true for us, but our quest is only beginning.

—*James B. Nelson*

In their need to perform men can lose touch with many other important things in life—friendship, solitude, love, childrearing.

—*Cris Evatt*

To really know a man, observe his behavior with a woman, a flat tire, and a child.

—*Anonymous*

What It Means to Be Male

Chalice Lighting

At times our own light goes out and is rekindled by a spark
from another person. Each of us has cause to think with deep
gratitude of those who have lighted the flame within us.

—*Albert Schweitzer*

Opening Words

Men today want to be playful, climb off the ladder,
celebrate our religious truths, confront our fears,
find rest and renewal, forgive and be forgiven,
learn from one another, children, women, and all the animals of
    the Earth.

We want to feel less miserable, unclench our fists,
open our tear ducts, face our own mortality.

We want to look upon life with gratitude,
feel celebration rising in our veins
leave a lasting legacy of thanks
for this gift of living.

—Tom Owen-Towle

Chant

There's a man in me, there's a man in you,
There's a woman in me, there's a woman in you,
There's a child in me, there's a child in you,
There's a god in me, there's a god in you.
And the man in me loves the man in you,
And the woman in me loves the woman in you
And the child in me loves the child in you
And the god in me IS the god in you.

—*Chief Eagle Feather*

Sharing Joys and Sorrows	*Please speak as you feel moved.*
Reading	"May I Be No One's Enemy" by Eusebius, Reading 521 in *Singing the Living Tradition*
Readings from the Common Bowl	*Take turns reading aloud.*
Sitting in Silence	In the quiet, may we be in touch with what we want to say to these people on this day.
Communing	*This is the heart of our service. Take turns sharing what you learned in preparing for today's gathering.*
Song	"From You I Receive," Hymn 402 in *Singing the Living Tradition*
Appreciations	*In a word or two, share how you feel about what happened at this gathering.*
Closing Words	We hold in gratitude all who have helped us to learn what it means to be male.

Readings from the Common Bowl

You are what your deep, driving desire is. As your deep, driving desire is, so is your will. As your will is, so is your deed. As your deed is, so is your destiny.
—*The Upanishads*

The male psyche has not been built upon the rational "I think therefore I am" but upon the irrational "I conquer; therefore I am."
—*Sam Keen*

Perhaps the time has come for a new agenda. Women, after all, are not a big problem. Our society does not suffer from burdensome amounts of empathy and altruism, or a plague of nurturance. The problem is men—or more accurately, maleness . . . . Men are killing themselves doing all the things that our society wants them to do. At every age they're dying in accidents, they're being shot, they drive cars badly, they ride the tops of elevators, they're two-fisted drinkers. And violence against women is incredibly pervasive. Maybe it's men's raging hormones, [or] . . . because they're trying to be a man."
—*from an article in* Newsweek

I talk when I should be listening to you, and when I should be talking about what is going on inside me I am quiet, with nothing to say. I am addicted to performance and winning, not simply because I have been conditioned this way, but also because my conditioning serves my present needs for defense. When I get the big contract or write the book or win the game I am in control, in charge of my life, and have influence over others.
—*James B. Nelson*

Are our images of what it means to be male changing? Are we the Frontiersman, the conqueror, —or the Healer . . . The Soldier, the defender, —or the Mediator . . . The Breadwinner—or the Companion . . . the Expert—or the Colleague . . . The Lord—or the Nurturer?
—*Mark Gerzon*

The deep nourishing and spiritually radiant energy of the male lies not in the feminine side, but in the deep masculine . . . . The kind of energy I'm talking about is not the same as macho brute strength . . . it's forceful action undertaken, not with compassion, but with resolve.
—*Robert Bly*

All real American men love to fight.
—*George S. Patton*

Men in America believe they are free. In reality, they are slaves of society's assumptions about what it means to "be a man." Throughout history these assumptions have supported aggression, conflict, and war.
—*Mark Gerzon*

I hold you at arm's distance. I become a reluctant revealer, an emotional evader because you might discover that at my core I am not really self-sufficient and strong. I am a terrifying mix of neediness and strength, of confusion and certainty, but that is hard to admit.
—*James B. Nelson*

You can get the fathering you need from any healthy man who is able and willing to give it.
—*John Friel*

Masculinity is not something given to you, something you're born with, but something you gain . . . . And you gain it by winning small battles with honor.

—*Norman Mailer*

Most social scientists would agree that there do exist striking similarities in standard male and female roles across cultural boundaries regardless of other social arrangements.

—*John Archer and Barbara Lloyd*

What a father says to his children is not heard by the world, but it will be heard by posterity.

—*Jean Paul Richter*

What should I do with my heroes? . . . Let your heroes become real people. . . . Don't make a god out of your hero. . . . See how they got there. . . . Know your limits and set realistic goals. . . . Find everyday heroes around you.

—*John Friel*

He cannot be a man without knowing how to be aggressive, but it must be controlled aggressions that is at his conscious disposal. If he is just overcome by his rage and violence, then it is no good; his masculinity is not yet found.

—*Robert Johnson*

Friendship, Partnership and Competition

Chalice Lighting

At times our own light goes out and is rekindled by a spark from another person. Each of us has cause to think with deep gratitude of those who have lighted the flame within us.

—*Albert Schweitzer*

Opening Words

May we be reminded here of our highest aspirations,
and inspired to bring our gifts of love and service
 to the altar of humanity.
May we know once again that we are not isolated beings
but connected, in mystery and miracle, to the universe,
to this community and to each other.

—*Anonymous*

Song

"From All That Dwell Below the Skies," Hymn 381 in *Singing the Living Tradition*

Sharing Joys and Sorrows

Please speak as you feel moved.

Reading

"We Need One Another," Hymn 468 in *Singing the Living Tradition*

Readings from the Common Bowl

Take turns reading aloud.

Sitting in Silence

In the quiet, may we be in touch with what we want to say to these people on this day.

Communing

This is the heart of our service. Take turns sharing what you learned in preparing for today's gathering. If you feel so moved, ask if anyone would like to be your coach as you work to find more balance in your life.

Song

"Love Will Guide Us," Hymn 131 in *Singing the Living Tradition*

Appreciations

In a word or two, share how you feel about what happened at this gathering.

Closing Words

We hold in gratitude all who have helped us to learn to be in friendship with one another.

Readings from the Common Bowl

I have also attempted to describe the intimacy of life in infantry battalions, where the communion between men is as profound as any between lovers. Actually it is more so. . . . It is, unlike marriage, a bond that cannot be broken by a word, by boredom or divorce, or by anything other than death. Sometimes that is not strong enough.

—*Philip Caputo*

It is no surprise that men often feel miserable. Look at the word; the hyphen tells the story: miser-able. Because we are stingy with our affections, tight with our time, pinched with our feelings, we fall prey to misery. The first dictionary definition of "miser" is "a wretched person."

—*Tom Owen-Towle*

I'm a self-made man, but I think if I had it to do over again, I'd call in others.

—*Roland Young*

All men are born equal but the tough job is to outgrow it.

—*Don Leary*

Don't walk in front of me, I may not follow. Don't walk behind me, I may not lead. Walk beside me and just be my friend.

—*Anonymous*

Friendship is a sheltering tree.

—*Samuel T. Coleridge*

Because I have been athirst I will dig a well that others may drink.

—*Arabian Proverb*

Behold, how good and pleasant it is when brothers dwell together in unity.

—*Psalm 133:1*

Be slow to fall into friendship, but when thou art in, continue firm and constant.

—*Socrates*

I dreamed in a dream I saw a city invincible to the attacks of the whole of the rest of the earth; I dreamed that it was the new city of Friends; Nothing was greater there than the quality of robust love.

—*Walt Whitman*

When a man becomes dear to me, I have touched the goal of fortune. I find very little written directly to the heart of this matter in books.

—*Ralph Waldo Emerson*

The question is not whether we think the same, believe in the same God, respond erotically to the same sex, but whether we are willing to stand for one another.

—*Kurt Kuhwald*

Self-disclosure is the one means, perhaps the most direct, by which self-alienation is transformed into self-realization.

—*Sidney Jourard*

But once the realization is accepted that even between the closest people infinite distances exist, a marvelous living side-by-side can grow up for them, if we succeed in loving the expanse between them, which gives them the possibility of always seeing each other as a whole before an immense sky!

—*Rainer Maria Rilke*

We need same-sex friends because there are types of validation and acceptance that we receive only from our gender-mates. There is much about our experience as men that can only be shared with, and understood by, other men. There are stories we can tell only to those who have wrestled in the dark with the same demons and been wounded by the same angels. Only men understand the secret fears that go with the territory of masculinity.

—*Sam Keen*

My friends have no friends. They are men. They think they have friends, and if you ask them whether they have friends, they will say yes, but they don't really. They think, for instance, that I'm their friend, but I'm not. It's OK. They're not my friends, either, the reason for that is that we are all men—and men, I have come to believe, cannot or will not have friends.

—*Richard Cohen*

Underneath all explanations for men's difficulty in friendship I believe there lies one pervasive and haunting theme: fear. Fear of vulnerability. Fear of our emotions. Fear of being uncovered, found out. So my fear leads to my desire to control— to be in control of situations, to be in control of my feelings, to be in control of my relationships. Then I will be safe. No one will really know my weakness and my vulnerability. No one will really know my doubts. No one will really know that I am not the producer and achiever I seem to be. Therein lies my real terror.

—*James B. Nelson*

I urge us men to pay heed to Jethro's advice to Moses, his son-in-law, to quit doing everything by himself and to invite others to share the responsibilities of his quest. When Moses turned for help, he learned that his burdens were cut in half.

—*Tom Owen-Towle*

Getting Centered and Balanced

Chalice Lighting

At times our own light goes out and is rekindled by a spark from another person. Each of us has cause to think with deep gratitude of those who have lighted the flame within us.
— *Albert Schweitzer*

Opening

Mindful of truth ever exceeding our knowledge
and community ever exceeding our practice,
reverently we covenant together,
beginning with ourselves as we are,
to share the strength of integrity
and the heritage of the spirit
in the unending quest for wisdom and love.
— *Walter Royal Jones, Jr.*

Song

"Gathered Here," Hymn 389 in *Singing the Living Tradition*

Sharing Joys and Sorrows

Please speak as you feel moved.

Reading

"Impassioned Clay" by Ralph N. Helverson, Reading 654 in *Singing the Living Tradition*

Readings from the Common Bowl

Take turns reading aloud.

Sitting in Silence

In the quiet, may we be in touch with what we want to say to these people on this day.

Communing	*This is the heart of our service. Take turns sharing what you learned in preparing for today's gathering.*
Song	"I Know This Rose Will Open," Hymn 396 in *Singing the Living Tradition*
Appreciations	*In a word or two, share how you feel about what happened at this gathering.*
Closing Words	May we leave tonight grateful for our sharing, giving thanks for the relationships we are forming here.

Readings from the Common Bowl

It is in deep solitude that I find the gentleness with which I can truly love my brothers. The more solitary I am the more affection I have for them. It is pure affection, and filled with reverence for the solitude of others.

—*Thomas Merton*

If I knew I was going to live this long I would have taken better care of myself.

—*Anonymous*

The purpose of life is simply to grow a soul.

—*A. Powell Davies*

All living growth is pliant until death transfixes it. Thus men who have hardened are "kin of death." And men who stay soft are "kin of life."

—*Lao-Tzu*

Why has play become the opposite of seriousness? It did not start out as such; it began as a natural way of being.

—*David Miller*

Every human being has a great, yet often unknown, gift to care, to be compassionate, to become present to the other, to listen, to hear and to receive. If that gift would be set free and made available, miracles could take place.

—*Henri J.M. Nouwen*

Simplicity, simplicity, simplicity! I say, let your affairs be as two or three, and not a hundred or a thousand.

—*Henry David Thoreau*

This day is mine.
May I remember this
and look for something new,
something perhaps I've stared at all my life
and never seen.

There's music and there's love and wit and
something that can lift
the mind.

May I discover these
and know the light's
not false and foreign
when I go
toward wonder.

—*Raymond John Baughan*

Each of us is an artist
Whose task it is to shape life
Into some semblance of the pattern
We dream about. The molding
Is not of self alone, but of shared
Tomorrow and times we shall never see.
So let us be about our task.
The materials are very precious and perishable.

—*Arthur Graham*

Our lives are like fragile eggs.
They crack and the substance escapes.
Handle with care!
Handle with exceedingly tender care
For there are human beings within,
Human beings as vulnerable as we are,
Who feel as we feel,
Who hurt as we hurt.

—*Richard S. Gilbert*

Let all hearts swell with glad acceptance,
joyful with the sense of the always becoming,
For out of earth, into the air and sunshine,
   out of ourselves,
There rises spirit in us. Neither dark nor threat
   shall thrust it down.
It rises irresistible in us.
This is the season's gift.

—*Robert T. Weston*

Making Amends

Chalice Lighting

At times our own light goes out and is rekindled by a spark from another person. Each of us has cause to think with deep gratitude of those who have lighted the flame within us.

—*Albert Schweitzer*

Opening Words

Holy and beautiful is the tradition that brings us together:
To face our ideals,
To remember our loved ones in absence,
To give thanks,
To make confession,
To offer forgiveness,
To be enlightened, and to be strengthened.
Let all our hearts prepare to open.

—*adapted from Robert French Leavens*

Song

"Amazing Grace!" Hymn 206 in *Singing the Living Tradition*

Sharing Joys and Sorrows

Please speak as you feel moved.

Reading

"A Litany of Atonement" by Robert Eller-Isaacs, Reading 637 in *Singing the Living Tradition*

Readings from the Common Bowl

Take turns reading aloud.

Sitting in Silence

In the quiet, may we be in touch with what we want to say to these people on this day.

Communing	*This is the heart of our service. Take turns sharing what you learned in preparing for today's gathering.*
Song	"There Is More Love Somewhere," Hymn 95 in *Singing the Living Tradition*
Appreciations	*In a word or two, share how you feel about what happened at this gathering.*
Closing Words	May we leave tonight grateful for our sharing, giving thanks for the opportunity to make amends, to begin again, and to deepen our relationships with one another.

Readings from the Common Bowl

A man must be big enough to admit his mistakes, smart enough to profit from them, and strong enough to correct them.

—*John C. Maxwell*

Our mistake is loving things and using people, when we should be using things and loving people.

—*Anonymous*

Unless I accept my virtues, I most certainly will be overwhelmed by my faults.

—*Robert G. Coleman*

Give a little love to a child, and you get a great deal back.

—*John Ruskin*

Grief is the doorway to a man's feelings.

—*Robert Bly*

There are two tragedies to life. One is not to get your heart's desire. The other is to get it.

—*George Bernard Shaw*

Push fears out the front door, disown them or try to conquer them by will power and they will only return by the back door, like rejected children seeking love. I am the father of my fears; they will only depart when I have learned to accept them.

—*Sam Keen*

All of my life I been like a doubled up fist—poundin', smashin', drivin'. Now I'm goin' to loosen these doubled up hands an' touch things *easy* with 'em.

—*Tennessee Willams*

Many men get more fun out of grinding the ax than in burying the hatchet.

—*Anonymous*

Forgiveness is not an impulse that is in much favor. The prevalent style in the world runs more to the high-plains drifter, to the hard, cold eye of the avenger, to a numb remorselessness. Forgiveness does not look much like a tool for survival in a bad world. But that is what it is.

—*Lance Morrow*

Perhaps the sexes are more related than we think, and the great renewal of the world will perhaps consist in this, that man and maid, freed from all false feeling and aversion, will seek each other not as opposites, but as brother and sister, as neighbours, and will come together as *human beings*.

—*Rainer Maria Rilke*

The most important thing a father can do for his children is to love their mother.

—*Anonymous*

Forgiveness is the final form of love.

—*Reinhold Niehbuhr*

I've looked on a lot of women with lust. I've committed adultery in my heart many times. This is something that God recognizes I will do—and I have done it—and God forgives me for it.

—*Jimmy Carter*

Nonviolence is the answer to the crucial political and moral questions of our time: the need for man to overcome oppression and violence without resorting to violence and oppression.

—*Martin Luther King, Jr.*

Like a bridge over troubled water I will lay me down.

—*Paul Simon*

To be ignorant of one's ignorance is the malady of the ignorant.

—*Bronson Alcott*

A journey of a thousand miles must begin with a single step.

—*Lao-Tzu*

You cannot have a proud and chivalrous spirit if your conduct is mean and paltry; for whatever a man's actions are, such must be his spirit.

—*Demosthenes*

Since we have not earned Bach—or crocuses or lovers—the best we can do is express our gratitude for the undeserved gifts, and do our share of the work of creation.

—*Robert R. Walsh*

If God appeared anywhere in the twentieth century —it was in the form of Martin Luther King, Jr.

—*David O. Rankin*

Family and Work

Chalice Lighting

At times our own light goes out and is rekindled by a spark from another person. Each of us has cause to think with deep gratitude of those who have lighted the flame within us.
—*Albert Schweitzer*

Opening Words

Spirit of Love, be with us tonight, as we join our lives once again to deepen our understanding and to kindle our compassion. Teach us to open to the possibilities of reconciliation and new beginnings. Remind us that what has been has been, and that what is to happen tomorrow depends in part on our choices. Help us to choose wisely, that we may be agents of your healing power. Be with us tonight in this gathering of men.

Song

"'Tis a Gift to Be Simple," Hymn 16 in *Singing the Living Tradition*

Sharing Joys and Sorrows

Please speak as you feel moved.

Reading

"For You" by Walt Whitman, Reading 659 in *Singing the Living Tradition*

Readings from the Common Bowl

Take turns reading aloud.

Sitting in Silence

In the quiet, may we be in touch with what we want to say to these people on this day.

Communing	*This is the heart of our service. Take turns sharing what you learned in preparing for today's gathering.*
Song	"Will You Seek in Far-Off Places?" Hymn 356 in *Singing the Living Tradition*
Appreciations	*In a word or two, share how you feel about what happened at today's gathering.*
Closing Words	May we leave tonight grateful for our sharing, giving thanks for insight into our lives with our families and with those with whom we work. In the spirit of love and reconciliation may we go forth, thankful for the opportunity to begin again and to deepen our relationships with one another.

Readings from the Common Bowl

Delight in your children openly. Give yourself, your humor, your small talk, and the minor affections of your hands and eyes. They aren't going to see many people who care . . . it would be nice if their father could be one.

—*Robert Capon*

Each night, when the fourteen to sixteen hours of drawing and painting were over, Vincent sat down with pen and ink and poured out his heart to Theo. There was no idea or thought too small, no happening too trivial, no element of his craft too insignificant, no scene too unimportant for Vincent to communicate to the only other living person who considered his every word and feeling precious.

—*Irving Stone*

What are dads good for? . . . to teach us how to win and lose, to begin and end things, to take risks and be safe with wisdom, how to be with men and women, how to learn from other men, to be a team player, how to surrender without being a wimp, to be spiritual, to guide and teach and lead, to like our bodies and have our feelings appropriately, to be political, and how to be committed.

—*John Friel*

Work is one of the greatest things in the world. So don't you think we should save some of it for tomorrow?

—*Anonymous*

The son of a rabbi went to worship on the Sabbath in a nearby town. On his return, his family asked, "Well, did they do anything different from what we do here?" "Yes, of course," said the son. "Then what was the lesson?" "Love thy enemy as thyself." "So, it's the same as we say. And how have you learned something else?" "They taught me to love the enemy within myself."

—*Andrew Schmookler*

It is easy to fly into a passion—anybody can do that—but to be angry with the right person to the right extent and at the right time and with the right object and in the right way—that is not easy, and it is not everyone who can do it.

—*Aristotle*

Without forgiveness life is governed . . . by an endless cycle of resentment and retaliation.

—*Roberto Assaglioli*

If you hate a person, you hate something in him that is a part of yourself.

—*Hermann Hesse*

Life is not a problem to be solved but a reality to be experienced.

—*Anonymous*

Extremists think "communication" means agreeing with them.

—*Leo Rosten*

We don't have time not to have time.

—*Gary Burke*

Nor did I ever tell him how close to him I felt that night—that for a little while the concrete wall between father and son had crumbled away and I knew that we were two lonely people struggling to reach each other.

—*Moss Hart*

There must always be a struggle between parent and child, while one aims at power and the other at independence.

—*Samuel Johnson*

Grief can take care of itself, but to get the full value of joy you must have someone to divide it with.

—*Mark Twain*

It is not always the great evils that obstruct and waylay our joy. It is our unnecessary and undignified surrender to the petty enemies: and I suggest it is our duty to scheme against them and make them subservient to human decree—time and schedules, our irritabilities of the day, and other worthy preoccupations. Matters more subtle and humane should command our lives.

—*Clarke Wells*

Life is too transient to be cruel with one another,
It is too short for thoughtlessness,
Too brief for hurting.
Life is long enough for caring,
It is lasting enough for sharing,
Precious enough for love.
Be gentle with one another.

—*Richard S. Gilbert*

Passion

Chalice Lighting

At times our own light goes out and is rekindled by a spark from another person. Each of us has cause to think with deep gratitude of those who have lighted the flame within us.

—*Albert Schweitzer*

Opening Words

Though our knowledge is incomplete, our truth partial, and our love imperfect, we believe that new light is ever waiting to break through individual hearts and minds to enlighten the ways of men, that there is mutual strength in willing co-operation, and that the bonds of love keep open the gates of freedom.

—*Napoleon W. Lovely*

Song

Praise love the quest we all may share;
Praise love and beauty everywhere;
Praise love the hope of good to be;
Praise love the truth that makes us free.

(to the tune of "Old Hundredth," Hymn 371 in *Singing the Living Tradition*)

Sharing Joys and Sorrows

Please speak as you feel moved.

Reading

"We Lift Up Our Hearts in Thanks" by Richard Fewkes, Reading 515 in *Singing the Living Tradition*

Readings from the Common Bowl

Take turns reading aloud.

Sitting in Silence	In the quiet, may we be in touch with what we want to say to these people on this day.
Communing	*This is the heart of our service. Take turns sharing what you learned in preparing for today's gathering.*
Song	"This Little Light of Mine," Hymn 118 in *Singing the Living Tradition*
Appreciations	*In a word or two, share how you feel about what happened at today's gathering.*
Closing Words	As our time together comes to a close, we give thanks for one another, for the chance to share our lives, and to renew our spirits in the company of friends. May we go forth enriched by our gathering, committed to living life fully, to loving life with more passion, and to supporting one another.

Readings from the Common Bowl

Fill me with anxiety, O Life!
Electrify me, make me nervous
Beyond any staid concern
For those things which challenge
Placid, flaccid ways, anachronisms of being.
Keep me tense, a-tiptoe,
Blinking at the novel,
Reaching out for those things
Just beyond my fingertips;
So that I may make patterns,
Dream dreams, fashion worlds
Which will beat with life.
For I would be a man
And on the move.

—*Arthur Graham*

Love is an unusual game. There are either two winners or none.

—*Anonymous*

O God, it's not your world, it's ours. Give us the courage to accept it, the grace to embrace it, the will to love it. Enable us, we pray, to appreciate and expand the moments of joy in life, whenever they come. Let them be for us bearers of hope which will enable us to endure any hour of despair, to the end that we, while the gift of life is ours, may help push back the dark with the flame of our faith.

—*Paul N. Carnes*

I would be silent and let infinity speak through me
To create in myself a greater patience
And passion
For our still unknown and undetermined ends.

—*Robert T. Weston*

Standing in the rain. Lying in the grass. Walking in the snow. Being present to our own breathing and the heartbeats of the person next to us. Approaching our lives with spontaneity, with a lack of self-consciousness, with simplicity. That's how we may experience our relationship to the force that gives us life.

—*Bruce T. Marshall*

Money can build a house, but it takes love to make it a home.

—*Anonymous*

Of all human passions love is the strongest, for it attacks simultaneously the head, the heart, and the senses.

—*Anonymous*

Nothing great was ever achieved without enthusiasm.

—*Ralph Waldo Emerson*

May you live all the days of your life.

—*Jonathan Swift*

Happiness is a healthy mental attitude, a grateful spirit, a clear conscience, and a heart full of love.

—*Anonymous*

When they are not close to their feelings, they may dismiss them as primitive, unsophisticated, and oversimplified.

—*Arthur Jonav*

Ask, and ye shall receive, that your joy may be full.

—*John 16:24*

Real joy comes not from ease or riches or from the praise of men, but from doing something worthwhile.

—*Anonymous*

You taught me to be nice, so that now I am so full of niceness, I have no sense of right and wrong, no outrage, no passion.

—*Garrison Keillor*

What do men want? . . . To feel, . . . to befriend, . . . to love, . . . to work, . . . to father, . . . to be whole, . . . and to heal.

—*John Friel*

The central demand of the body is to be felt.

—*Arthur Jonav*

Men are taught not to show feelings because it's unmanly, a sign of weakness.

—*Jonathan Kramer*

This is the day which the Lord has made. Let us rejoice and be glad in it.

—*Psalms 118:24*

Loving Relationships

Chalice Lighting

At times our own light goes out and is rekindled by a spark from another person. Each of us has cause to think with deep gratitude of those who have lighted the flame within us.

—*Albert Schweitzer*

Opening Words

Where in our hearts is
That burning of desire?
  It is true that we are made of dust
  And the world is also made of dust,
  But the dust has motes rising.
Whence comes that drive in us?
  We look to the starry sky
  And love storms in our hearts.
Whence comes that storm?
  The journey of love is a very long journey.
But sometimes with a sigh you can cross that vast desert.
  Search and search again without losing hope;
You may find sometimes a treasure on your way.

—*Mohammed Iqbal*

Song

"There Is More Love Somewhere," Hymn 95 in *Singing the Living Tradition*

Sharing Joys and Sorrows

Please speak as you feel moved.

Reading

"These Roses" by Ralph Waldo Emerson, Reading 556 in *Singing the Living Tradition*

Readings from the Common Bowl	*Take turns reading aloud.*
Sitting in Silence	*In the quiet, may we be in touch with what we want to say to these people on this day.*
Communing	*This is the heart of our service. Take turns sharing what you learned in preparing for today's gathering.*
Song	"We Would Be One," Hymn 318 in *Singing the Living Tradition*
Looking Ahead	*Reflect together on whether this group should meet again. When? Where? Who will lead?*
Appreciations	*In a word or two, share how you feel about what happened at today's gathering.*
Closing Words	For this community of men we are grateful. For the opportunity to listen and to learn we feel gratitude. For the making and deepening of friendships we give our thanks.

For this community of men we are grateful.
For the opportunity to listen and to learn we feel gratitude.
For the making and deepening of friendships we give our thanks.

May we go forth holding each other in our hearts.
May we support one another on our journeys as men.
May we each grow as friends, as partners, as lovers.

In the days and weeks to come, let us strive to balance our lives,
to offer and receive forgiveness,
and to bring more love and passion to the world.

Readings from the Common Bowl

Everything in the household runs smoothly when love oils the machinery.

—*Anonymous*

He who grasps loses.

—*Lao-Tzu*

Love cures people, both the ones who give it and the ones who receive it.

—*Karl Menninger*

Goethe came to the astounding observation late in his life that the province of man is to serve woman; then she will serve him. He was talking about the inner woman, the muse.

—*Robert Johnson*

Men's need for independence makes them sensitive to being engulfed by others who want connection or intimacy.

—*Cris Evatt*

If you want great wealth, and that which lasts
     forever, Wake up!
If you want to shine with the love of the Beloved,
     Wake up!

—*Jalaluddin Rumi*

Love does not dominate; it cultivates.

—*Johann Wolfgang von Goethe*

It is impossible to express love with a clenched fist.

—*Anonymous*

At the heart of love, there is a simple secret: the lover lets the beloved be free.

—*D. James Kennedy*

Love is always patient and kind; it is never jealous; love is never boastful or conceited; it is never rude or selfish; it does not take offense, and is not resentful. Love takes no pleasure in other people's sins but delights in the truth; it is always ready to excuse, to trust, to hope, and to endure whatever comes.

—*1 Corinthians 13:4-7*

Love wakes much and sleeps little, and, in sleeping, does not sleep. It faints and is not weary; it is restricted in its liberty yet is in great freedom. It sees reason to fear, and does not fear, but, like an ember or a spark of fire, flames always upward.

—*Thomas a Kempis*

Love came and it filled me with the Beloved. . . .
Now all I have is a name, the rest belongs to the Beloved.

—*Jalaluddin Rumi*

It is not surprising that we keep looking for love, because we are born of love. We come out of love. All of us are nothing but vibrations of love. We are sustained by love, and in the end we merge back into love. . . . This world is nothing but a school of love; our relationships with our husband or wife, with our children and parents, with our friends and relatives are the university in which we are meant to learn what love and devotion truly are.

—*Swami Muktananda*

Eros invites the experience of the holy. It encourages men to loosen their grip on the need to control, and that is both its attraction and its fearfulness. Eros is longing. At its deepest it is the urgent longing of our whole being for communion and connectedness. . . . Sometimes it appears through . . . flesh's longing for flesh, and should that loving result in orgasm, for a delicious moment we are thrown out of control. It is the experience men both seek and fear. Intimacy does not thrive on patterns of control. It does thrive when control needs are relaxed, when deep desire for connection is admitted. That is an invitation to the holy.

—*James B. Nelson*

The Lover is ever drunk with love. . . .
He dances with ecstasy and delight.

—*Jalaluddin Rumi*

All of a sudden tears began to flow from my eyes,
And I was filled with a desire to find the one whom everyone adores.

—*Nazir*

What It Means to Be Male

Think back through your life journey to three people or events that have influenced your notion of what it is to be male. List them here.

Visualize an important moment with one of these persons or events. Write about or draw where you are. What is the surrounding area like? Who is there? What is happening?

Remember the reactions you had. What were your feelings? How were you affected?

What do these experiences show you about what it means to be a man?

What discoveries would you like to share in the next gathering?

Preparation for Gathering Three
Friendship, Partnership and Competition

Think of three different ways you interacted with men in the last few days: one instance in which you were friends, one in which you were in partnership, and one in which you were competing.

For each of these three roles, draw a circle. Make the size of the circle reflect the relative amount of time you spend in that role. In each circle, write key words that come to mind when you are in that role. Include words about feelings, values, actions, opinions, attitudes, images, power exercised, and learnings.

Describe the ways each of these feed or starve your soul.

Name the feelings and discoveries you would like to share.

Please write on a separate piece of paper a quotation (including the author) or a poem or song related to the topic for Gathering Three, and add it to the Common Bowl.

Getting Centered and Balanced

Draw a circle in the middle of this page, and write your name in it. Draw five more circles around the center circle. Think of the five most important people you spoke to in the last few days, and write one name in each of these circles.

Draw arrows from the circle representing you to each of the five circles and arrows from each of the five circles back to you. The arrows pointing toward you represent what you are receiving from these other people. Write some words on these arrows that reflect your predominant feelings about how the other person affects you. These feelings can be positive or negative. The arrows pointing away from you reflect what you give the other people. At the head of these arrows, write your predominant feelings about what you bring to each relationship. Does what you give deplete or energize you? Now look at the overall interaction between you and these five people. How do you feel about it? Write a few words expressing your impressions about this interaction.

Shade in the circle above that represents the person who creates the most stress for you. Then find the person who gives you comfort and joy and draw a little heart next to their circle. For the most important interactions, ask yourself what feelings you would like to have and write them down near the arrows between you and that person. Select the relationship that is most important to you. Ask yourself what it would take to get from where you are to where you would like to be with this person. Write down what you will do in the next two weeks to move toward where you want to be.

Write on a separate sheet of paper a short sentence or find a quotation (including the author) that reflects an important message related to the topic for Gathering Four. Bring it to the gathering and add it to the Common Bowl.

Making Amends

At a quiet moment, ask yourself, "Whom have I significantly harmed?" Write his or her name below. If more than one person comes to mind, write down the name of the person you are most willing to focus on in this exercise.

Write an apology to this person. In your apology:
- explain what you regret having done or not done
- express empathy and acknowledge the injustice you caused
- clearly accept total responsibility for your action or inaction, without blaming anyone else or making excuses for yourself
- tell what you are sincerely willing to do to correct the harm you have done, either by offering restitution or by promising not to repeat the behavior

If you cannot correct the harm done without causing further harm to yourself or the other person, read your apology aloud to yourself and then destroy it. Write down some ideas about how you can forgive yourself. If you can correct the harm done without causing further harm to yourself or others, consider making the amends you've described within the next two weeks.

Write a short sentence on a separate piece of paper or find a quotation (including the author) that reflects an important message related to the topic for Gathering Five. Add it to the Common Bowl.

Family and Work

For this exercise, do a nonrepresentational drawing. This type of drawing contains shapes, lines, and colors, but not anything you would recognize, such as trees or houses or people.

Sitting quietly, take five deep, slow breaths and clear your mind of the activities surrounding you. Think about what you do with your family and what you do not do. Think about what you do at work and what you do not do. Just take some time to be with those thoughts and feelings related to family and work. Turn to the next page and, without thinking about what you are doing, select a crayon or marker with your non-dominant hand. Let your hand move freely across the page. If you find yourself trying to create an image, stop and free your mind of any thoughts before you continue. Draw until you feel that you have finished.

At the top of the page, write a title for this drawing. At the bottom of this page, write down a few feelings you had as you were drawing and that you are now feeling as you write. Write down what your drawing seems to be telling you.

Find the part of the drawing that seems most compelling to you. Write down what seems to be happening there. Do the same for other sections of the drawing.

Draw a circle below. As you review your drawing and comments, write key words in the circle that refer to the difficulties you have revealed. Underline the five words reflecting the areas where you are experiencing the most stress.

Select one of the stressful areas you identified on the previous page and imagine what you can do to create some relief. Be realistic, but stretch a little. Write a plan stating what you will do in the next two weeks to handle this situation. Be specific about when, where, and how you are going to handle this.

Write a short sentence on a separate sheet of paper or find a quotation (including the author) that reflects an important message related to the topic for Gathering Six. Bring it to be offered to the Common Bowl.

Passion

Draw a circle and label it "Joy." Inside the circle, write all the things you can think of that ignite joy in you.

Draw another circle and label it "Harmony." Inside the circle, write all the things you can think of that would give you a sense of harmony.

Draw another circle and label it "Sex." Inside the circle, write all the things you can think of that would make you feel sexy.

Draw another circle and label it "Support." Inside the circle, write all the things you can think of that would give you a feeling of being supported.

In each of the above circles, underline the three items that speak to you the most. Select one of the underlined items from each circle. Write a one-sentence commitment to make each of these things happen and describe how you will do so. Be very specific.

Write on a separate sheet of paper a short sentence or find a quotation (including the author) that reflects an important message related to the topic for Gathering Seven. Offer it to the Common Bowl.

Loving Relationships

In this exercise, focus on a present or a past loving relationship. Please adapt the questions to your situation.

Looking at this relationship, what have you done really well?

In what ways were you good at asking for what you wanted?

What more could you have done to ask for 100 percent of what you wanted, 100 percent of the time?

In what ways do you think you could have paid better attention to the relationship?

In what ways could you have better shown that you appreciated your partner?

What did you discover about yourself in doing this exercise? What would you do differently in the future?

Response Form

Rate how valuable you found each part of Gatherings, using the following scale:
1 = not very   2 = somewhat   3 = moderately   4 = very   5 = extremely

Topics

____ Getting to Know One Another

____ What It Means to Be Male

____ Friendship, Partnership and Competition

____ Getting Centered and Balanced

____ Making Amends

____ Family and Work

____ Passion

____ Loving Relationships

Format

____ Opening Words

____ Song

____ Sharing Joys and Sorrows

____ Reading

____ Readings from the Common Bowl

____ Sitting in Silence

____ Communing

____ Song

____ Preparing for the Next Meeting

____ Sharing Feelings or Appreciations

____ Closing Words

____ Exercises

If a friend asked you what this small-group ministry for men was like, what would you say?

Overall, what did you like about Gatherings?

When, if ever, did you feel that anything inappropriate happened?

What would you like to see done differently? Be as explicit as you can.

What other topic(s) would you like to see included?

What topic(s) do you think could be replaced?

In what other ways could we improve Gatherings?

Please write additional comments here.

If you would be interested in co-leading a Gatherings group, please tell the group leaders.

Suggestions for Leaders

Leading a small group, particularly one that encourages open and honest sharing of the deepest things that are on our minds and in our hearts, is both a challenge and a blessing. You may wonder if you are really prepared to handle the sensitive topics that arise. Our experience is that men will go as deep as they are comfortable with and no deeper. This depth needs to be honored for whatever it is. All you need to do is respect the individual's feelings and hold them empathically. The blessing is that this can become a spiritual moment in which hearts meet and growth occurs. The group's trust is a gift that they give to you. Preparing well for each gathering and attending to practical details is more than an administrative task; your work helps the group to focus on each other and on what is being offered and received rather than on logistics.

Inviting Participants

Because some men would like to feel more included in congregational life, we recommend sending a personal letter of invitation to all the men in your congregation, including recent visitors. It should describe the Gatherings format and topics, and specify where and when the eight gatherings will be held. A sample is provided on page 56. Men registering for the program should provide contact information.

The ideal size of the group is eight to twelve. A larger group limits the amount of sharing time for each participant. If more than the maximum number register, you can create a waiting list for the next Gatherings program.

Preparation

Choose a quiet meeting space, free from interruption, where chairs can be placed in a circle around a low table set with a cloth and a chalice. The chalice may be lit before participants arrive. Before the gathering, copy the quotations, adding any you want to include. Cut them apart, and place them in a small bowl or basket on the table. Also obtain copies of *Singing the Living Tradition* for all of the participants.

Have all your preparations completed before the first participant arrives so that you are able to welcome each man and let him know you are glad he is there.

After Each Gathering

A few days after each gathering, remind participants about their take-home exercise. This will discourage last-minute preparation and deepen their experience. Contact any men who were not able to participate, tell them they were missed, and ask them to come prepared to the next gathering.

Invite Feedback

We hope that the men in your group will find Gatherings a meaningful experience and will want to continue. Photocopy the Response Form on pages 52-53 and distribute them during the "Looking Ahead" part of Gathering 8. Invite participants to share their feelings about Gatherings and turn the forms in to you at their convenience. Written feedback will be very helpful if your group decides to keep meeting. If the group chooses new leaders, give them the response forms.

Thank You

Your commitment to serve as leaders is a gift to your men's community. We hope that you find the leadership experience rewarding. May you touch the hearts of the men in your Gatherings group and be ministers to them.

Invitation Letter

Dear Men of [congregation],

We hope you will be part of Gatherings, an eight-meeting program that will consider topics particularly important in men's lives. We will be sharing thoughts, experiences, doubts, and beliefs. Each week, we will follow an Order of Service with a time of sharing as the central element. Appreciative listening is at the core of Gatherings.

Here is our plan:
What: Gatherings
When: [Day, time, dates]
Where: [Location]
Leaders: [Names]

    [Date]   Getting to Know One Another
    [Date]   What It Means to Be Male
    [Date]   Friendship, Partnership and Competition
    [Date]   Getting Centered and Balanced
    [Date]   Making Amends
    [Date]   Family and Work
    [Date]   Passion
    [Date]   Loving Relationships

In advance of each gathering some preparation will be needed. For the first gathering, to help us get to know one another, please bring a few magazine pictures or photographs reflecting an interesting, exciting, or meaningful time in your life.

Gatherings will be a good way to explore personal experiences, beliefs, and possibilities, and a great way to get to know other men of the congregation. Although there is no fee, you do need to register. To do so, please call the church office at [phone number].

We hope you will join us.

[signatures]